One

1 - 5

6 - 10

Two

Three and Four

Our Family

Five

Six

Seven

Eight

Nine

Ten

Snacking

Brushing

Dressing

Reading

Taping

Our Bedtime Tour

Waiting

Goofing

Fishing

Ant

Duck

Boating

10 Minutes till Bedtime

PEGGY RATHMANN

SCHOLASTIC INC.
New York Toronto London Auckland Sydney
Mexico City New Delhi Hong Kong

ISBN 0-439-13376-9

12 11 10 9 8 7 6 5 4 3 2 1   0 1 2 3 4 5/0

Printed in the U.S.A.   08

First Scholastic paperback printing, September 2000

Lettering by David Gatti

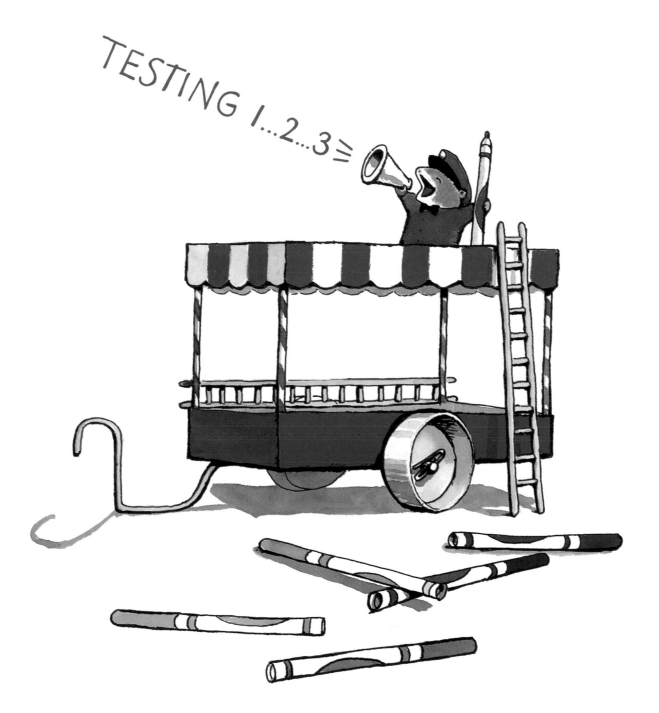

potty

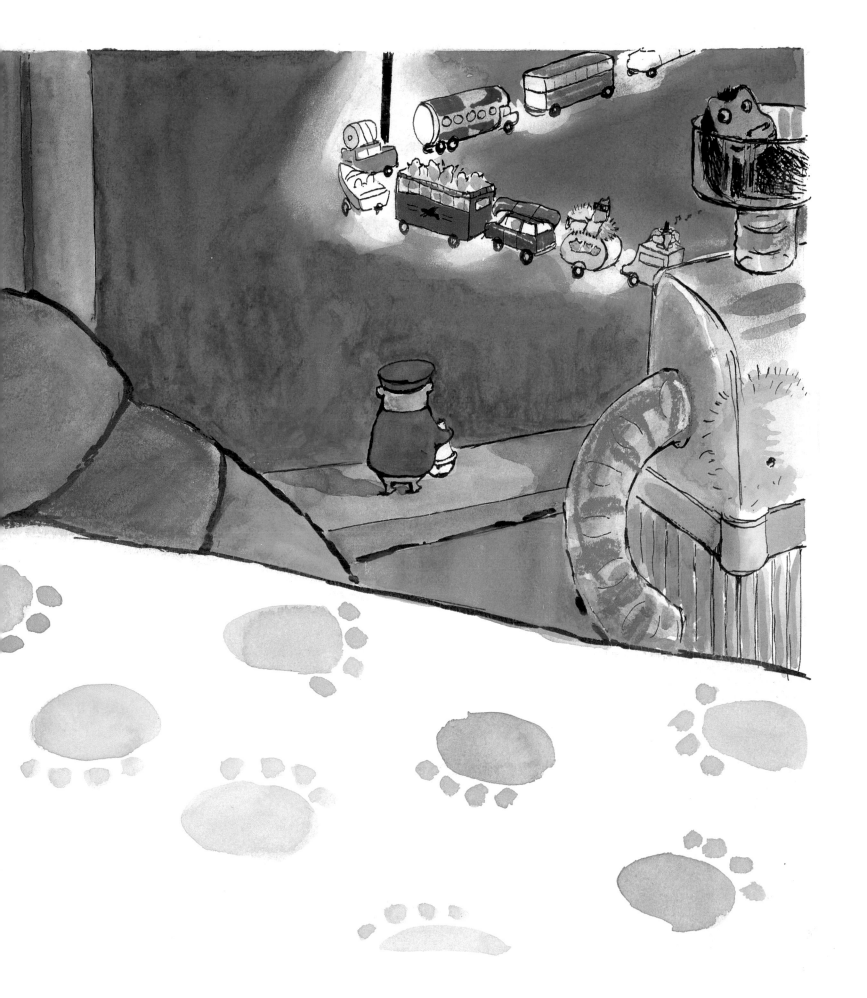